WEST COUNTRY PLACE-NAMES AND WHAT THEY MEAN

Avon, Somerset and Wiltshire

by
CYRIL DAVEY

ABSON BOOKS · ABSON · WICK · BRISTOL

First published in Great Britain in 1983
by ABSON BOOKS, Abson, Wick, Bristol

ISBN 0 902920 53 7

Printed at the Burleigh Press, Bristol, England

THE ORIGINS

This booklet is by no means a study of our place-names in this part of the West Country, but only an indication of how they came into existence. It points to one of the most fascinating parts of our heritage, and fills a gap because when I looked for a simple booklet on the subject I could find none. It could not, of course, have been written without constant reference to the classic *Concise Oxford Dictionary of English Place-Names* though it is not a mere transcript of it. If you want to study the subject in more detail there may well be books in your local library. Eilert Ekwall's authoritative book which I have mentioned is indispensable and *The Origin of English Place-Names* by P. H. Reaney (Routledge, Kegan Paul) will provide most of the background.

Begin by remembering one fact. All names mean something. Very few of our town or village names are new or even recent. Even a name like Weston-super-Mare, which sounds like the invention of a classically-minded Victorian town-publicist, is more than seven centuries old. Probably more than three-quarters of the names in these counties are over a thousand years old. But in order to find what lies behind them you need some history, a little knowledge of what the countryside looked like before the Norman Conquest of 1066, and preferably some information about social, community and religious life.

First, then, a brief summary of West Country history.

The people of the Iron Age, which began in Britain about 500/600 BC, were not merely 'our forefathers dressed in skins'. The tools, weapons and ornaments in your local museum will

1

show that they, within their limits, were cultured and possessed of notable skills. It is to these people, and perhaps to the later Bronze Age before them, that we owe great historic monuments ('prehistoric' is a quite misleading word) like Stonehenge, Avebury and Silbury, as well as the fortified 'camps' on many of our hills, such as the various 'Cadburys'.

Then, from 500 BC onwards, came the massive Celtic invasions from continental Europe. They were a culturally-advanced people, warlike and expansionist, with strong tribal organisation and a form of society which included a land-owning 'aristocracy'. They conquered southern England by taking possession of it, and moved as far west as Cornwall and Wales, and in those two countries remained comparatively undisturbed by the succeeding invasions from the continent. 'Celt' – a title cherished in Wales and Cornwall – is seldom used of the rest of the country. These Celtic settlers were the British people, and the land they took over became known as Britain.

About the beginning of the Christian era the Roman empire was at its most vigorous. Julius Caesar's invasion had begun the conquest of Britain and between AD 45/50 Vespasian, who was himself later to be emperor, subjugated Wiltshire and set up Roman rule in the west. For the most part throughout Britain Roman authority was beneficent rather than harsh, with strongly-built towns and an administration that left a great deal of autonomy to the British themselves. Indeed, many of the Celto-British aristocracy took over a Roman way of life, including no doubt building themselves villas in imitation of the Roman farmer-settlers.

The Roman peace lasted for some four hundred years in Britain, until Rome itself came under pressure. Then, as its empire began to crumble under attacks from expanding tribes such as the Goths and Huns, the legions were withdrawn from Britain in AD 425. The withdrawal was the signal for attack by the Germanic tribes, especially the Angles and the Saxons who had already made marauding forays from AD 360 onwards. Now they came in force and by 450 were established on the upper Thames and on the Severn. The magnificent British revival led by 'king' Arthur between 505 and 538 was no more than a last stand by the old British resistance and had no real significance. Britain became the country of the new conquerors – Wessex the country of the West Saxons, for instance, as Sussex and Essex were of the South and East Saxons. Britain itself became England – the land of the Angles and Saxons. This time, however, the conquerors were not like the Romans who ruled on behalf of a distant emperor, and stood apart from local life; the Saxons took over the land with its villages, towns, farms and stock, made them all their own, and for the most part appear to have subjugated the inhabitants ruthlessly.

Nevertheless life settled into normality and England was to enjoy some six centuries of freedom from invasion, except for a brief period of Danish war and kingship, before its most thorough and final foreign conquest. The Danes, who tried to subdue England in the 9th century, were resisted in the west by King Alfred – first being defeated by them and finding shelter in Athelney and then making more decisive war which resulted in the 'peace of Wedmore'.

Not until 1066 was the country again invaded, this time by William, Duke of Normandy. In the main the Norman Conquest was a peaceful take-over of Saxon England, moving it more firmly into European life, culture and politics.

It is not easy to visualise the countryside of Wiltshire and Somerset in the Saxon and early Norman era. Like a great deal of southern England, Wiltshire was covered with dense forests and through them ran twisting streams and small rivers, many of them now dried up or diverted, with bog and marshes on their sides. The great uplands, which we know as Salisbury Plain and its associated downs, must have been much the same then as now, except for the thick forest dwindling into scrub woodland on their lower slopes. The undulating hills and forests continued into what is now Gloucestershire and up to where

Bristol now stands; but beyond the Mendips the vista changed completely. Here the vast areas of flat land were completely submerged in still water, with small 'islands' standing above it, and causeways running across it just above water-level. Though in summer the marshes dried out to some extent, the higher parts bearing willow and rushes, it was not properly drained for many centuries. Westwards were the coastal hills, the Brendons and the Quantocks, and beyond them the small fishing villages and ports of the Channel.

The life of the people was conditioned by the type of country they lived in, with fishermen in the watery meres of Somerset and on the coast, and most of the remaining areas given over to agriculture. Larger towns grew up by the rivers, though by our standards they were no more than substantial villages, with farmland round them. There, and in most of the open spaces in the forests, cereals were grown and cattle, sheep, pigs and goats raised. Diet was supplemented by hunting, mainly for deer despite the fact that they were normally the preserve of the landowners. There was little sense of 'community' except a very local one. Farms and villages were isolated from each other, good roads hardly existed, and the main communication-paths were between the bigger towns or from the villages to the markets. The farm or the 'manor' was the dominant feature of any village or hamlet; and labourers, craftsmen such as woodworkers or smiths, and ancillary 'professionals' like hunters or horse-breeders, all depended on the patronage of the farmer or landowner.

• • •

So – how does this political and social history, and the type of the country itself, affect our place-names?

A modern analogy will help us to see how names grew up. If someone asks you the way to a certain place you might well answer him something like this. 'Follow this road 'til you come to Wilson's garage, turn left and go on until you come to a pond and then turn right past Peter Holway's farm. Just beyond the kennels you'll get to the main road'.

Your directions would have included personal names – the garage and the farm; a recognisable natural feature – the pond; and an occupational centre, the kennels. It was precisely by using such symbols that all our place names were created.

The Bronze and Iron Age peoples left nothing of their language behind them and none of our place-names go back to that period. Nevertheless the 'memorials' they left – the monoliths and standing-stones, the burial-mounds and especially the fortified hill-camps – were to be used by their successors, the British Celts, to describe their own place and these were built into our names.

In Wiltshire and Somerset British place-names are rare for their Saxon conquerors must quickly have wiped the British speech out of existence. Nevertheless we know something of what the language was like. It was to survive as Welsh in Wales and as Kernou in Cornwall, both of them British nations in areas which the Saxons never over-ran. The remnants of British names in our own area do, however, provide some odd situations. Why, for instance, did the Saxons not give new names to the rivers? That they did not do so is clear, for almost all the river names are British. *Avon* is still the Welsh word for river, and amongst the rest Axe is almost the same as Exe in Devon, Usk in the Welsh border-country and Esk in the north.

Maen is a Welsh word for hill and so is *crug*. The British must have used the same words two thousand years ago, for *maen* crops up as *men* in various places. The most obvious is the Mendips – the dip or cleft in the hills. On the Somerset coast was a headland-hill – a *men*. Over the years it got changed to *mine* and later settlers added another-word – *head*. Minehead is really, therefore, hill-head or headland-headland. The same thing happened with Churchill. It has nothing to do with a church. It is really *crug* or *creech,* a cognate British word, and both mean hill. So Churchill is really *crug*-hill, or *creech*-hill – *hill*-hill.

Burg or *burh* appear to come from a British word for encampment which was used to describe the Iron Age hill-forts throughout the west country. The ancient peoples of the hut-circles and hill-camps are recalled in dozens of the names which end with *burg, burh* or *bury.*

Four hundred years of Roman occupation left hardly any stamp on our place-names in these counties, though Cirencester is the Roman 'Corinium' and Gloucester, a little to the north, is 'the splendid shining place near the Roman fortress'. Apart from Bath there are only two main Roman remains amongst our names – the Roman fortress-town and the Roman road. *Castra,* the Latin word for a fort, appears for instance in Ilchester – the Roman *castra* or fortress on the river Gifl, itself a British river-name. There were two great Roman roads down which the legions marched through Wiltshire or Somerset – the Fosse Way and Ermine Street. *Strada* was the Latin word for 'road', becoming 'street' in English. Street itself was built on, and perhaps on both sides of, the great Roman road. Ditcheat is 'the place by the gap (*yat*) in the Ditch' – in other words 'in the Fosse Way' for the Fosse Way cut through the undulating hills like a huge ditch or dyke.

But the vast majority of our place-names date from Saxon times; they are the real 'English' names. Though the 'dictionary' which follows explains the meaning of many of them it is useful here to indicate the main ways in which they arose. You will recall the reference on page 5 to the way we tend to direct someone to the place he wants to find; we use personal names, natural features and occupational places. These were amongst the commonest ways in which the Anglo-Saxons described their own places. From Cornish and Welsh place-names it is clear that the British almost always used topographical features to differentiate their farms and villages –

hills, lakes, valleys, promontories and so on – but hardly ever used personal names. The Saxon English on the other hand used personal names a great deal. Very many of our villages have the name hidden in them of an early tenant or landowner who has been dead for forty generations.

Nailsea, for instance, has nothing to do with the sea. *Ea, ei* or *ey* meant island. Nailsea was Nagel's island, standing above the Somerset marshes. In the same way Tissa was an English farmer who worked his land near an old British *burg* or encampment, and give his name to Tisbury.

Sometimes, however, the name commemorates the family rather than the person himself. The English word *ing* (sometimes shortened to *en*) which crops up in so many names means family or extended family of brothers, sisters, cousins and so on or even dependents on the farmer. Tockington is the farm (*tun*) of Tocca's family (*ing*); Tickenham is the homestead of Ticca's family and workpeople.

But the English, like the British before them, very often used natural features. Barlinch is the ridge where the barley grows; Wambrook is the crooked stream; Mark is the place where a boundary-stone stood.

Religion played some part in the formation of names, too. Though 'church' is in one or two cases a corruption of the British *crug* or *creech* (hill) it mostly means exactly what it says. As the 'heathen' Saxons settled down and became the English they were Christianised by missionaries working their slow and dangerous way through the forests infested with wild animals and over the lonely hills and downs. Small churches were erected in some villages, though other newly-Christian families no doubt worshipped in the farm-house itself or in the open air. In some cases farmers put up their own churches and left a permanent memorial behind – Pucklechurch is a reminder that a farmer, Pucca, built his own church here for his own family and workers.

Most of these early Saxon churches were no doubt made of

mud and wattle and did not stand for more than a century or so but in the towns, small though they then were, stone churches were erected as time went on. Most of these disappeared, too, or were used for other purposes – like the famous Saxon church at Bradford-on-Avon. Parts of some others were incorporated into the new Gothic churches built by the Normans. A minster, a word occurring quite frequently, was literally a monks' church and might mean a larger church built by a group of monks or even a monastery, though it sometimes seems to be used merely to describe a rather larger church-building.

The Danish invasion brought a substantial Scandinavian element into the place-names of northern and eastern England but they had little effect on west-country life and none at all on our place-names. *By, thorp, toft* and *thwaite,* so common in Yorkshire or Lincolnshire, for instance, are not found anywhere in our own local names.

By the 11th century England had been settled for five hundred years by the Anglo-Saxons. Countryside, custom and language were all their own. Then came the almost bloodless Norman Conquest under a well-organised, well-armed force led by Duke William of Normandy who was to become William I, the Conqueror. Norman-French became the refined language of the court and the ruling classes but for the ordinary Englishman there was no significant change in speech. He continued to use English and although the passing centuries have made his speech and writing unintelligible to modern Englishmen it remained the basic framework, and until a hundred years ago provided much of the vocabulary, of our own English language.

The Normans did not invent new names for old towns, villages or farms, as the Saxons had done. Their only real contribution to our place-names came through changes of ownership. Where a Norman baron or land-grabber took over an English manor or estate his own name tended to be added to it, and there are a great many evidences of this custom in Wiltshire and Somerset. In this way Brompton – the farm where the broom grew, or perhaps the farm near the Brendon Hills became Brompton Ralph when it passed into the ownership of Ralph Fitz Urse, who was already connected with Dunster, in 1245. In some cases, too, ownership passed to the now strongly-organised Church and an ecclesiastical name was added. Thus Canna's family-home became Bishops Cannings when it came into the possession of the Bishop of Salisbury.

From the point of view of place-names, however, one event soon after the Norman Conquest was of outstanding importance. William I undertook the first comprehensive survey and census of the whole of his new kingdom. Armies of clerks travelled, sometimes perilously, through the nation and noted down every town, village and farm of consequence, often with the names of their occupiers, sometimes of their dependants and their various occupations. The result was the massive series of reports known as the Domesday Book. The census-takers, of course, had problems. The English were often illiterate and unable to spell even their own names. The census-men were French and found it hard to understand what they regarded as the rough language of the English who even had letters in their written words which did not occur in the Norman alphabet. They did their best but the names, as they set them down, were seldom spelt as they were in such English historic documents as the Anglo-Saxon Chronicle dating a couple of hundred years before the Domesday Book.

Sometimes the differences were not very great. The English spelt a town Wiltun in the Anglo-Saxon Chronicle; the Normans wrote it down as Wiltune in the Domesday Book. At other times the difference was extreme. The English reported to the census-taker that the name of his village was Ciselburg; the Norman must have been more obtuse than usual for he put down in the Domesday Book the name Ceoselbergon. This is an example not only of the difference between English and Norman but of the way time has dealt with both of their names; in our own time it has become Chiselborough.

9

Through the careful script of the writers of the Domesday Book, despite all the language problems they tried to puzzle out, one startling fact stands out. More than half the place-names of Wiltshire, Somerset and Avon appear in the Domesday Book. Its date is 1086.

The majority of our towns, villages and hamlets have been in existence for well over a thousand years.

• • •

It is certainly possible to get a fairly clear idea of what some places used to be, indeed of what many places were, because the same old English words appear so often in our place-names. 'English' means that they all come from what used to be called 'Anglo-Saxon', and when you find any of them in a place-name that, in itself, points to the fact that the farm, cottage, stream, village or whatever the place was, existed in that spot at least a thousand years ago.

By remembering what these common elements mean it is easy to begin to picture the place behind the name. They normally follow a personal or descriptive name or word.

Some obvious elements

The words in this list all meant just what they do today:
bridge; *brook*; *down* (in the sense of high, open land); *field*; *ford*: *ridge* (of a hill-side); *well* (though in the sense of a spring rather than a well that has been constructed); *wood*.

Some possibly misleading elements

In some cases it is easy to be misled because the element or word does not mean what it now means or the original Anglo-Saxon word has ceased to exist in modern English. Here are some of the commonest misleading elements.

church. (1) In the earlier pages it has been pointed out that this

10

is sometimes derived from the Celtic/British word for 'hill' – *crug*, which is occasionally rendered *church* or *creech*. (2) It should be remembered that where the word means church, as it normally does, the building would have been very simple, small, roughly-built in the early period of Saxon Christianity and will certainly have disappeared centuries ago.

cliff may sometimes only mean a steep slope near the sea or a river, rather than high cliffs in our modern sense.

cot is cottage but often cottages were no more than wattle or clay-and-reed buildings, or even wooden huts.

gate is very misleading because it does not have our modern sense at all. It comes from *yat* which means gap, either a gap in the hills or perhaps in the surrounding woodlands.

minster can sometimes mean monastery, though in many cases it would be no more than a centre where only a few monks lived rather than a large establishment. It was also used, apparently, to describe a church larger than usual.

red can often mean red in colour, but at other times it is a shortening of reed or reedy.

Elements that often occur

Those that follow are very familiar but very few of them are used in their original sense and most of them we do not use at all today.

-bourne: a stream or small river.

-burgh, burh, bury. All the same word. They refer to a fortification. In most cases this was a British camp or walled or ditched enclosure, often on a hill or rising ground. The word can also mean a fortified manor.

-chester, cester or *caster*: from the Latin *castra*, a Roman fortress.

-comb, combe, or *coom*: a valley.

-den: valley.

-don: hill.

-ey or *ea*: island.

-ham: one of the commonest word-endings which must have

11

had a wide variety of meanings all related to the idea of people living together – a homestead, a village, an estate or a manor. The word usually follows a personal name.

-hamtun, hamton, hampton: probably the village proper, as distinct from the village and the scattered houses round about it.

-ing, -en: always follows a personal name and means 'the family of'; it is usually the middle element in a word which ends in either *ham* or *tun* (i.e. the village/farm of the family of . . . .

-lea, leh, ley: usually an open space in woodland or forest, used for pasturage or farming.

-stock, stoke: first meant holy place; then meeting place; later came to be used of a farm on that site.

-ton, tun: not always easy to distinguish in meaning from *ham*, but it is often taken to mean farm, or village dominated by a farm.

-worth: enclosed homestead or farm.

-wic, wich, wych: could be dwelling, house, or even village, but often appears to have meant dairy-farm.

A

THE COUNTY NAMES

Avon: is a common British river-name from a Celtic word meaning water.

Somerset: the *saete*, which means tribe or people, who lived at Somerton. Somerton itself means the *tun* (farm or village farming-area) to which the people moved only during the summer months.

Wiltshire: the administrative area related to Wilton. Wilton was the *tun* (farm or village) on the river Wilye.

THE PLACE-NAMES

A – Avon. S – Somerset. W – Wiltshire.

[DB] – the place is mentioned in the Domesday Book, 1086.

A **Abbots Leigh:** woodland farm belonging to the Abbot (of St Augustine's, Bristol).

W **Abbotston:** manor held by the Abbess of Wilton.

A **Abson:** manor of the Abbot of Bath and Gloucester.

W **Aldbourne:** Ealda's family stream. *[DB]*

W **Alderbury:** fortified place where Aethelwaru lived. *[DB]*

S **Alford:** the ford of Aeldgyth. *[DB]*

W **All Cannings:** the old place where Cana's family lived. *[DB]*

A **Almondsbury:** where Aelhmund lived, by the old camp. *[DB]*

W **Alton Barnes:** farm near the course of the R. Avon, later held by the Berners family from Bernieres, Normandy.

W **Alton Priors:** as above, held by the Priory of St Swithin, Winchester.

W **Alvediston:** Aelvith's farm.

A **Alveston:** Alwih's farm. *[DB]*

W **Amesbury:** Amber's home near the British camp. *[DB]*

A - B

w   **Ansty:** narrow footpath (usually on a hillside). *[DB]*

s   **Ashcott:** cottage by the ash-trees. *[DB]*

s   **Ashill:** hill where the ash grows. *[DB]*

w   **Ashton Gifford:** farm where the ash-trees grow; held in 1242 by Elias Giffard – his name comes from Old French word meaning bloated.

A   **Long Ashton:** long village by the ash-trees.

A   **Rood Ashton:** farm by the ash-trees, with old cross nearby. *[DB]*

A   **Steeple Ashton:** as above, where the church had a steeple on the tower. *[DB]*

s   **Athelney:** the island of the aethlings (Saxon princes). *[DB]*

w   **Atworth:** Atta's farm.

A   **Aust:** was mentioned in 794 in connexion with Auston, an unknown person who may have lived much earlier, possibly a Roman named Augustus. *[DB]*

w   **Avebury:** Afa's home near the British camp. *[DB]*

A   **Avon:** a Celtic/British river name, from the word for water.

A   **Avonmouth:** exactly what it says, a very modern name.

w   **Avoncliff:** steep-sloping ground on the river Avon.

s   **Axbridge:** bridge over the river Axe – British river name from same root as Exe, Esk and Usk, linked with a word for water.

s   **Babcary:** Babba's home on the river Cary – a British water-name. *[DB]*

A   **Backwell:** the stream coming from the ridge. *[DB]*

s   **Badgworth:** Baega's farm enclosure.

A   **Badminton:** the farm of Baedamund's family. *[DB]*

s   **Bagborough:** Bacga's hill. *[DB]*

w   **Bagshot:** the gap in hills/woods where Beocc lived. *[DB]*

s   **Baltonsborough:** Bealdhun's hill or barrow. *[DB]*

s   **Bampton:** farm of the dwellers by the warm spring. *[DB]*

A   **Banwell:** Bana's spring or, possibly, the felon's spring. *[DB]*

S **Barle:** British name of a river or stream.

S **Barlinch:** ridge of hill where the barley grew.

S **Barrack:** barley-farm, probably on the edge of the farm or estate.

A **Barrow Gurney:** the wood-grove; later held (1086) by Nigel de Gurnai. *[DB]*

A **Bath:** the place of the Roman baths. *[DB]*

A **Bathampton:** the farm of the people by the warm spring. *[DB]*

A **Batheaston:** the eastern farm. Bath was added much later. *[DB]*

S **Bats Castle:** iron-age fort where bats were found.

W **Baverstock:** Babba's dairy-farm. *[DB]*

W **Baydon:** hillside where berries grew.

S **Bayford:** land held by peasants, probably rented from landowner

A **Bedminster:** monastery or church founded by monk Beda – (*not* Venerable Bede). *[DB]*

W **Bedwyn:** place where convolvulus grew. *[DB]*

W **Bemerton:** the farm of the trumpeters. *[DB]*

S **Berrow:** the hills, or mounds.

W **Berwick Bassett:** corn farm; held in 1212 by Alain Bassett (Norman name means short stature).

W **Biddestone:** Bieda's farm. *[DB]*

A **Bishopston:** the bishop's manor.

A **Bishopsworth:** the bishop's homestead-farm. *[DB]*

W **Bishops Cannings:** Canna's family place; later held by Bishop of Salisbury.

S **Bishops Hull:** hill-manor, held by Bishop of Winchester.

W **Bishops Lavington:** Lafa's farm; later belonged to Bishop of Sarum. *[DB]*

W **Bishops Lydeard:** seems to be a Celtic/British name, Litgart, as owner; later owned by Bishop of Wells.

A **Blaise:** very uncertain but seems to be a personal name.

S **Blagdon:** black hill.

B

w **Boscombe:** valley were the box-trees grew. *[DB]*

w **Bottlesford:** ford by Bota's place.

s **Bower Hinton:** cottage by the farm on high land.

w **Box:** the box-trees. *[DB]*

w **Bradford-on-Avon:** broad ford over the Avon. *[DB]*

w **Brail:** park stocked with deer for hunting.

w **Bratton:** the newly-cultivated farm. *[DB]*

s **Brendon Hill:** brown-coloured hills. *[DB]*

s **Brean:** a British word for headland. *[DB]*

s **Brent Knoll:** British word implying a steep place. *[DB]*

s **Bridgehampton:** the bridge by the big village.

s **Bridgwater:** the bridge of Sir Walter de Douai. *[DB]*

w **Brinkworth:** Brynca's enclosed farmstead. *[DB]*

A **Brislington:** Beorhthelm's farm.

A **Bristol:** the place where the bridge was. *[DB]*

w **Brixton Deverill:** Beorhtric's farm on the river Deverill coming down from the fertile uplands. *[DB]*

w **Broad Chalke:** wide, open limestone uplands.

w **Broad Hinton:** open space near the farm on high land

s **Broadway:** the wide road. *[DB]*

s **Broadwood:** the great woods. *[DB]*

A **Brockley:** the open space in the woods, by the brook. *[DB]*

w **Brokenborough:** the broken hill – i.e. the valley or gap in the hill. *[DB]*

s **Brompton Ralph:** farm by the Brendon Hills; held in 1245 by Ralph Fitzurse. *[DB]*

s **Brushford:** ford by the bridge. *[DB]*

s **Bruton:** farm on the river Brue. *[DB]*

s **Buckland Sororum:** (or Minchin Buckland) land held by charter with a nunnery.

w **Budbury:** Budda's place by the iron-age stone circle or fort.

w **Bugley:** might be a goblin's glade, or Bugge's glade.

w **Bulbridge:** bullock's bridge.

w **Burbage:** the brook from the hillside.

s   **Burnham:** the farm on the stream. *[DB]*

A   **Burrington:** the farm by the hill.

W   **Buttermere:** land by lakeside, giving good butter. *[DB]*

AWS **Cadbury:** Cada's place by the iron-age fort.

W   **Cadnam:** Cada's people's village.

s   **Calcote:** hut for calves.

W   **Calcutt:** hut where charcoal was kept. *[DB]*

W   **Calne:** British name for the river. *[DB]*

s   **Cannington:** farm on the Quantocks. *[DB]*

s   **Carhampton:** farm on or near the rocks. *[DB]*

s   **Castle Cary:** iron-age fort on the river Cary (British river-name). *[DB]*

W   **Castle Combe:** valley with British fortification.

W   **Castle Eaton:** farm by river with fort nearby. *[DB]*

s   **Catcott:** Cada's cottage. *[DB]*

s   **Chaffcombe:** valley where calves were kept. *[DB]*

W   **Chalfield:** the cold field. *[DB]*

s   **Chalvey:** calves' enclosure, or possibly island with calves.

s   **Chapel Allerton:** Christian chapel, built at Aelfwerda's farm. *[DB]*

W   **Chapmanslade:** merchants' valley.

s   **Chard:** rough common-land. *[DB]*

W   **Charlcote:** cottage of the churls (peasants free of duties to lord of manor).

W   **Charlton:** the churls' (free peasants) farm. *[DB]*

s   **Charlton Adam:** churls' farm; held by William FitzAdam, 1206. *[DB]*

s   **Charlton Mackrell:** churl's farm; held by Makerell family (Norman name taken from the fish). *[DB]*

s   **Charlton Musgrove:** churl's farm; granted to Richard de Mucegros in King John's reign. *[DB]*

A   **Charterhouse-on-Mendip:** Priory of Carthusian monks, founded 1243.

s   **Cheddar:** the ravine. *[DB]*

C

A   **Chelwood:** Ceola's wood. *[DB]*

S   **Chesterblade:** iron-age camp, perhaps built in shape of a leaf.

W   **Cheverell:** the roe-buck. *[DB]*

A   **Chew:** British river-name.

A   **Chew Stoke:** dairy-farm on river Chew. *[DB]*

A   **Chewton Mendip:** farm on river Chew, near the Mendips. *[DB]*

A   **Chilcompton:** farm in the valley belonging to the son/ child of a nobleman. *[DB]*

W   **Chilhampton:** home-farm of the children – probably older sons of a nobleman.

W   **Chilmark:** pole, used as a boundary mark. *[DB]*

W   **Chippenham:** village of Cippa's family. *[DB]*

A   **Chipping Sodbury:** the market held at Soppa's place by the hill or iron-age fort. *[DB]*

S   **Chipstable:** Cippa's home, with a large post by it. *[DB]*

W   **Chisbury:** Cissa's place, near the iron-age camp. *[DB]*

W   **Chisenbury:** Cissa's home, near the iron-age fort. *[DB]*

S   **Chiselborough:** the place with gravel, near the fort or hill. *[DB]*

W   **Chiseldon:** the gravel valley. *[DB]*

W   **Chitterne:** the house in the woods. *[DB]*

W   **Chittoe:** the yew-woods.

W   **Cholderton:** the farm of Ceoldred's family. *[DB]*

A   **Churchill:** from British *crug*, meaning hill; thus 'hill-hill'.

W   **Chute:** woods, a British word.

W   **Chute Forest:** Forest added by Saxons to word Chute which they did not know really meant forest already.

S   **Clanville:** clean-field – not French ville but Saxon vil.

S   **Clatworthy:** enclosed farmland where the burdock grew. *[DB]*

A   **Claverham:** village where there was clover. *[DB]*

A   **Claverton:** farm, where clover grew. *[DB]*

A   **Cleeve:** cliff or hill-slopes. *[DB]*

A   **Clevedon:** hill with cliffs. *[DB]*

A   **Clifton:** farm on the cliffs.

S   **Cliffe Pypard:** sloping ground; held by Richard Pipart in 1231. French name meaning piper. *[DB]*

A   **Clutton:** farm on hillside. *[DB]*

W   **Coate:** cottage.

W   **Codford:** the ford by Coda's home.

S   **Coker:** British name of the stream. *[DB]*

W   **Colerne:** house where charcoal was kept or made. *[DB]*

W   **Collingbourne Ducis:** old name for the upper R. Bourne; held by the Earls, later Dukes, of Lancaster. *[DB]*

W   **Collingbourne Kingston:** as above; farm belonging to the king.

    Compton: the farm in a valley – a common name; many of these farms were taken over by Norman barons and landowners, as below.

W   **Compton Bassett:** valley farm taken over by Fuke Basset, 1242. *[DB]*

S   **Compton Bishop:** as above, belonged to Bishop of Wells.

W   **Compton Chamberlayne:** as above; Galfridus Camerarius, 1234. *[DB]*

A   **Compton Dando:** as above; de Alno family in 12th century. *[DB]*

S   **Compton Dundon:** valley farm by the hill (no reference to Norman owners). *[DB]*

S   **Compton Durville:** see Compton; held by Eustachius de Dureuill, 1230. *[DB]*

A   **Compton Greenfield:** as above; Richard de Greinvill, 1228. *[DB]*

A   **Compton Martin:** as above; son of Martin de Tours in reign of Henry I.

S   **Compton Pauncefoot:** Richard Pauncefoot – French word meant round belly. *[DB]*

A   **Congresbury:** place where St Congar was buried, c. AD 1000, the founder of the church here, near the iron-age hill-fort. *[DB]*

C - D

W   **Conrish:** farm with the cows.

A   **Combe Down:** the downs above the valley.

S   **Corfe:** gap in the hills.

W   **Corsham:** Cusa's village. *[DB]*

S   **Creech:** British word for hill, barrow, ridge or mound.

S   **Crewkerne:** house on the spur of the hill. *[DB]*

S   **Cricket:** small hill or mound, British word crug. *[DB]*

W   **Cricklade:** gate leading to the woods.

S   **Crowcombe:** valley where the crows were found. *[DB]*

W   **Crudwell:** Credda's spring.

S   **Cucklington:** farm of Cucol's family. *[DB]*

     Curry: British name for the river.

S   **Curry Load:** road by the Curry Stream.

S   **Curry Mallet:** held by William Malet – French word means evil. *[DB]*

S   **Curry Rivel:** held by Richard Rivel, 1194 – French word means rebel.

W   **Damerton:** the farm of the judges. *[DB]*

W   **Dauntsey:** island belonging to someone whose name began with 'D' but is not traceable. *[DB]*

W   **Deptford:** deep ford. *[DB]*

W   **Devizes:** place on the boundary (devize). A 12th century castle stood here on the boundary of two hundreds (administrative districts).

A   **Didmarton:** Didda's farm, on a boundary. *[DB]*

S   **Ditcheat:** the gap in the dyke; the dyke/ditch was the Roman road, the Fosse Way. *[DB]*

W   **Ditteridge:** ridge near the Fosse Way – the ditch. *[DB]*

A   **Dodington:** farm of Dodda's family. *[DB]*

S   **Doulting:** black river or dirty river, an old name for R. Sheppey. *[DB]*

S   **Dowlish:** the dirty or black river. *[DB]*

W   **Drake:** the place of the dragon, a reference to local folklore.

s **Draycott:** cottage on a steep slope where things had to be dragged up. *[DB]*

s **Dulverton:** farm by the hidden ford. *[DB]*

A **Dundry:** the steep ascent of the ridge.

s **Dunkery:** a Celtic hill-name.

s **Dunster:** Dunn's hill. *[DB]*

A **Dyrham:** enclosure for deer. *[DB]*

A **Easter Compton:** the sheepfold on the valley-farm.

w **Easton Grey:** the eastern farm; held by Johannes Greiz, 1242. *[DB]*

w **Ebbesbourne Wake:** the Ebble was a British river-name; held by Galfridus Wac, 1166. *[DB]*

A **Ebdon:** Ebbe's hill.

w **Ebsbury:** Ebba's place at or near the hill, probably with an iron-age fort.

w **Eisey:** the island where a pre-Christian god was worshipped. *[DB]*

w **Etchilhampton:** the farm of the people on the oak-covered hill. *[DB]*

s **Evercreech:** hill with the yew-trees. *[DB]*

s **Exford:** the ford over the river Exe. Exe is a British river-name. *[DB]*

A **Farrington Gurney:** farm on fern-covered ground, held by Robert de Gurnai, 1225. *[DB]*

w **Farleigh:** fern-covered glade. *[DB]*

s **Farnborough:** fern-covered hill. *[DB]*

w **Faulston:** Fallard's farm.

s **Feltham:** village where hay was grown or harvested.

w **Figheldean:** Fygla's valley. *[DB]*

A **Filton:** hay farm.

A **Fishponds:** the ponds where fish were found or stored.

s **Fitzhead Bavant:** for Fitzhead see Fivehead; held by Roger de Bavent, 1316.

F - G

s **Fivehead:** an area of five hides. One hide was reckoned to be the area of ground sufficient to maintain a family.

w **Flamston:** Flambard's farm; held by Walter Flambard, 1227. Unusual to find a Norman name attached to the Saxon word for farm.

A **Flax Bourton:** farm by the fortified manor; flax was added later, from the fact that flax was later cultivated there.

s **Foddington:** farm where grazing-fodder was kept or grown. *[DB]*

w **Fonthill Bishop:** where the River Font (old British river-name) flowed down from upper fertile regions; owned by Bishop of Winchester, 901. *[DB]*

w **Fonthill Gifford:** as above; held by Berengar Gifard, 1086.

s **Forscote:** the fox's earth. *[DB]*

w **Fosbury:** uncertain but suggested that it means the hill of the old chieftain. *[DB]*

w **Fovant:** Fobba's spring. *[DB]*

w **Foxham:** village where foxes were common.

w **Foxley:** fox wood. *[DB]*

A **Frampton Cotterell:** farm on river Frome; held by Adam Cotella, 1167. *[DB]*

A **Frenchay:** woods on the river Frome.

A **Frogland Cross:** froggy land, probably where paths crossed.

s **Frome:** British river-name. *[DB]*

w **Froxfield:** froggy stream.

s **Galhampton:** the village where the rent-paying peasants and their families lived.

s **Galmington:** the farm of the rent-paying peasants.

w **Gastard:** a narrow tongue of land where goats were kept.

s **Gawbridge:** bridge by the home of rent-paying peasants.

w **Giddeahall:** Gydda's ford.

s **Glastonbury:** place where woad grew by the old hill

22

(glassy island is a mis-translation of the old British name). *[DB]*

s **Goathurst:** goat-wood. *[DB]*

s **Godney:** Goda's island; possibly a reference to the island where a pre-Christian god was worshipped.

s **Golsoncott:** the goldsmith's village.

s **Goose Bradon:** Bradon is a British name of uncertain meaning; held by Norman family, de Gouiz. *[DB]*

A **Gordano:** Latinised form of old British Gor-Danu – muddy valley.

W **Grimstead:** homestead in the green fields. *[DB]*

A **Hallatrow:** holy tree. *[DB]*

s **Halse:** place on a neck of land. *[DB]*

A **Hambrook:** the rocky, or stoney, brook.

W **Hanging Langford:** the long ford by the slope of the hill.

W **Hardenhuish:** huish comes from a word meaning sufficient land to support a family; here it was in a valley where hares were found. *[DB]*

A **Harptree:** tree where the harpers lived, met or played. *[DB]*

A **Hartcliff:** slopes where stags were found.

W **Hartham:** enclosure for deer. *[DB]*

s **Haselbury Plucknett:** the hazel grove; held by Alan de Plugenet, 1268. *[DB]*

W **Hawthorn:** grey thorn-trees.

A **Hawkesbury:** where Hafoc lived by the old fortified hill. *[DB]*

W **Heddington Wick:** the village where Hedda's people had a dairy-farm. *[DB]*

s **Hele:** a corner.

A **Henbury:** high hill.

s **Henstridge:** ridge of the hill where stallions were kept. *[DB]*

s **Hescombe:** the valley where the witch lived. *[DB]*

H - I

AS   **Hewish:** see Hardenhuish.

S   **Highbridge:** the high bridge.

S   **Hillfarrance:** the hill; held by Robert Furon, 1182. *[DB]*

A   **Hinton Blewett:** farm on high land; held by Norman family, Bleuet, meaning blue. *[DB]*

A   **Hinton Charterhouse:** highland farm; Carthusian priory founded here 1232. *[DB]*

S   **Hinton St George:** highland farm; church was dedicated to St George. *[DB]*

SW   **Holt:** woodland.

S   **Holton:** farm in a remote valley.

S   **Holway:** sunken road.

W   **Honeystreet:** Huna's home by the Roman road.

S   **Honeywick:** dairy-farm, where honey was made, or Huna's dairy farm.

A   **Horfield:** dirty field.

S   **Hornblotton:** farm of the horn-blowers. *[DB]*

W   **Horningsham:** village on the spur of the hill. *[DB]*

S   **Horsey:** horse-island. *[DB]*

S   **Horsington:** farm of the horse-keepers or horse-breeders. *[DB]*

W   **Hullavington:** Hunlaf's family's farm.

S   **Huntscott:** Hunter's cottage.

S   **Huntworth:** enclosed homestead where the hunts lived.

S   **Huish Champflower:** (see Hardenhuish); held by Thomas de Chanfleur, 1212.

S   **Huish Episcopi:** as above; held by Bishop of Wells.

S   **Hurcot:** huntsman's hut.

S   **Ilchester:** the Roman fortress on river Gifl —early Celtic name for R. Yeo. *[DB]*

S   **Ilminster:** monastic church on river Gifl. *[DB]*

W   **Inglesham:** Ingin's village.

W   **Ingst:** probably a British river-name.

S   **Isle Abbots:** Isle is not island but a corruption of British

24

river-name, river Gifl was an early Celtic name for R. Yeo. Belonged to Muchelney Abbey. *[DB]*

A **Itchington:** farm on river Icene (cf this British river name with Itchen).

W **Keevil:** wood where they found timber for barrels and tubs. *[DB]*

S **Keinton Mandeville:** (really 'Kingston'), royal manor; held in 1201 by William de Maundvill. *[DB]*

A **Kelston:** village where calves were reared.

A **Kenn:** British river name.

W **Kennet:** as Kenn.

A **Keynsham:** Caegin's village. *[DB]*

S **Kingsbury Episcopi:** the king's manor by the hill; held by Bishop of Bath.

S **Kingsdon:** hill-pasture belonging to the king.

S **Kingston Pitney:** Pitt's island on the king's manor.

S **Kingston St George:** the king's manor; church dedicated to St George.

A **Kingston Seymour:** king's manor, with name of later family holding it. *[DB]*

A **Kingswood:** the king's wood.

W **Knighton:** the farm belonging to the lord's steward. *[DB]*

S **Knole:** hillock/knoll.

A **Knowle:** as Knole.

W **Lacock:** the little stream. *[DB]*

W **Langford, Hanging:** the long ford on, or below, the slope. *[DB]*

W **Langford, Steeple:** as above, where the church had a steeple. *[DB]*

W **Langley Burrell:** long clearing in the woods; held later by Petrus Burel. *[DB]*

A **Lansdown:** Long ridge of downland.

S **Lattiford:** the beggars' ford or vagabonds' ford. *[DB]*

L - M

A   **Lawrence Weston:** the western farm; church dedicated to St Lawrence.

A   **Laverton:** farm where larks were plentiful.

W   **Leigh Delamere:** cleared glade in the forest; held by Adam de la Mare, 1242.

S   **Liscombe:** valley with a pig-sty.

W   **Littleton Drew:** small farm; held by Walter Drew, 1242. *[DB]*

W   **Littleton Pannell:** small farm; held by Wilelmus Painel, 1242. *[DB]*

W   **Lockeridge:** ridge with an enclosure for animals on it.

W   **Longbridge Deverill:** the long bridge on the river then known as the Devrel. *[DB]*

W   **Longleat:** the long stream.

S   **Lopen:** Lufa's sheep-fold.

W   **Lover:** Leofhere's house.

S   **Luccombe:** possibly Lufa's valley, but the usually staid *Oxford* book suggests it may be 'the valley where lovers went'. *[DB]*

W   **Ludgershall:** cave where spears were set to trap animals.

W   **Ludwell:** stream that made a loud noise.

S   **Lullington:** Lulla's farm.

A   **Lulsgate:** the gap in hills or forest where Lulla lived.

A   **Lydiard:** A British hill-name.

W   **Lydiard Millicent:** the name of an early woman owner. *[DB]*

S   **Lydiard St Lawrence:** the dedication of the church.

W   **Lydiard Tregoze:** held by Robert Tregoz in 12th century. *[DB]*

W   **Maiden Bradley:** a hospital for women at the monastery in the broad glade in the forest. *[DB]*

A   **Mangotsfield:** Mangoda's field. *[DB]*

W   **Manningford Abbots:** ford where Manna's family lived; held by Abbey of St Peter, Winchester.

w **Manningford Bohune:** as above; held by Henry de Boun, 1310. *[DB]*

w **Manningford Bruce:** as above; held by a Norman family named Bruce. *[DB]*

s **Mark:** the boundary stone.

w **Market Lavington:** Laffa's family's farm; where a regular market was held.

w **Marlborough:** the hill, probably with a British camp, where Maerle lived. *[DB]*

A **Marshfield:** the field that was marshy or was by a marsh.

w **Marston:** farm by the marsh.

s **Marston Bigot:** marshy farm; held by Richard de Bigot, 1195. French word means bigotted. *[DB]*

w **Marston Maisey:** the marshy farm; held by Roger de Meysi, 1213.

s **Martock:** the farm-enclosure by the lake. *[DB]*

s **Meare:** the lake – Domesday Book mentioned 10 fishermen living on it. *[DB]*

w **Melksham:** the farm where the cows gave very good milk. *[DB]*

s **Mells:** the mills. *[DB]*

AS **Mendips:** the hills (cp Welsh *maen* for the British hill-word) with a cleft through them.

w **Mere:** the lake. *[DB]*

s **Merriott:** the gate on the boundary. *[DB]*

s **Middlezoy:** the middle part of the river. Zoy is one form of a British river-name). *[DB]*

A **Midsomer Norton:** the northern farm or village; where the church was dedicated to St John, whose festival is held on Midsummer Day.

s **Milborne:** the mill-stream. *[DB]*

s **Milton:** the middle farm. *[DB]*

s **Milverton:** the farm by the ford with the mill. *[DB]*

s **Minehead:** from British word for hill (cp Welsh *mynydd*), and headland. *[DB]*

M - N

W **Minety:** island in the stream, where mint grew.

S **Misterton:** farm with a monastery.

S **Monksilver:** monks from Goldhill in Monmouthshire settled here on a very clear stream.

S **Montacute:** the pointed hill. A late name, from Norman French owners or tenants. *[DB]*

S **Muchelney:** the large island. *[DB]*

S **Mudgley:** the muddy meadow.

A **Nailsea:** Nagel's island.

S **Namansland:** no man's land.

W **Neigh Bridge:** Bridge at an island. Saxon-English for island is ei or ey; 'at an ei' became nei, as, 'at an ash' or 'at an oak' became Nash and Noakes.

S **Nempnett:** place at or by the plain (plain is emnett and the name comes, as above, from at an emnet.

W **Netherhampton:** the lower part of the big village.

S **Nether Stowey:** the lower part of the paved road (Over S- is the upper part).

S **Nettlecombe:** valley with nettles.

W **Netton:** the cattle farm.

A **Newton St Loe:** the new homestead; passed into ownership of Roger de Sancto Laudo, 1122. *[DB]*

S **Neroche Forest:** the nearby place where hunting dogs were kept, by or in the forest.

S **Northover:** the place on the northern bank of the R. Yeo.

W **Norton Bavant:** the northern farm; held by Roger Bavant, 1344. *[DB]*

S **Norton Fitzwarren:** as above, with family name of Norman owner. *[DB]*

A **Norton Hawkfield:** as above; the Norman owner was Hauteville. *[DB]*

A **Norton Malreward:** as above; held by William Malreward, 1235. *[DB]*

S **Norton St Philip:** as above; church dedicated to St Philip.

s **Nunney:** the island with the nunnery. *[DB]*

s **Nynehead:** nyme is a corruption of nine, and head of hide – the estate extending to nine hides of land. A hide was the land considered necessary to support one family.

s **Oake:** where the oak-trees grew. *[DB]*

w **Oare:** British river-name (cf Eyre and Syr). *(DB)*

w **Oaksey:** Wocc's island. *[DB]*

w **Odstock:** Odda's stock; see note on Stock/Stoke. *[DB]*

w **Ogbourne:** the stream where Occa lived. *[DB]*

A **Olveston:** Aelf's farm.

w **Orcheston:** Odric's farm.

w **Orcheston St George; St Mary:** as above, with church dedications.

s **Otterhampton:** the large village but otter seems to be a personal name rather than a reference to the mammals. *[DB]*

s **Over Stratton:** the farm above the Roman road.

A **Parkway:** the road by the park-land or estate.

A **Patchway:** the road by Paecca's home.

A **Paulton:** the farm on the high ridge.

s **Paxcroft:** Paecca's smallholding.

A **Peasedown St John:** the downs where the wild peas grew; church dedication.

s **Pendomer:** the hill (pen is British word); name of Norman owner, possible Domere or Dunmere. *[DB]*

s **Pennard:** from the British word for high hill. *[DB]*

s **Penselwood:** two British words meaning the great wood on the hill. *[DB]*

A **Pensford:** the pig-sty by the ford.

s **Petherton, North and South:** farm on the river Parrett (British river-name). *[DB]*

w **Pewsey:** Pefe's island. *[DB]*

A **Pilning:** the creek.

s **Pilton:** the farm on the creek. *[DB]*

P - R

S **Pitminster:** the church, perhaps founded by monks, on Pippa's land. *[DB]*

W **Pitton:** Pitta's farm.

S **Porlock:** enclosed land by the harbour. *[DB]*

A **Portbury:** the hill, possibly with British camp, by the harbour. *[DB]*

A **Portishead:** the harbour-village under the ridge. *[DB]*

W **Potterne:** the potter's house. *[DB]*

W **Poulshot:** Paul's wood.

S **Poundisford:** the ford by the pinder's house. A pinder was a man whose task was impounding stray cattle.

S **Preston Plucknett:** the farm of the priests; held by Alain de Plugenet, 1268. *[DB]*

A **Priddy:** British word for earth or soil, presumably possible for cultivation on the rocky land of the Mendips.

S **Puckington:** the farm with the goblins. *[DB]*

A **Pucklechurch:** the church build on Pucela's land. *[DB]*

S **Puriton:** the farm with the pear-trees. *[DB]*

A **Puxton:** Puckerell's farm (name of a Norman rather than English owner).

S **Pylle :** the creek. *[DB]*

S **Quantocks:** British word cantoc meaning ridge of hills.

S **Quantoxhead:** the high point of the ridge.

S **Quarne:** the mill.

A **Queen Charlton:** churl's farm; given to Catherine Parr by Henry VIII.

W **Quemerford:** the ford at Cynemer's place.

W **Quidhampton:** the big village where Cwida lived.

A **Radstock:** enclosed farmland by the road, i.e. the Fosse Way. *[DB]*

W **Ramsbury:** the hill, possibly with a British camp where ravens lived. *[DB]*

A **Redcliffe:** where the red ground sloped down to the river.

A   **Redland:** the cleared land, for agriculture, probably.

SW   **Redlynch:** the marsh with the reeds. *[DB]*

A   **Redwick:** the dairy-farm where reeds grew. *[DB]*

W   **Rodbourne:** the stream where the reeds grew.

A   **Rood Ashton:** the farm with the ash-trees where there was a village cross.

W   **Rowde:** the reed-beds. *[DB]*

W   **Rushall:** the bank, possibly at the roadside where travellers rested.

W   **Salisbury:** the meaning is apparently impossible to disentangle successfully because the original place-name was Sarum, and both name and ecclesiastical centre were transferred to the new place. *[DB]*

W   **Salterton:** the salt-workers' or salt-makers' farm.

S   **Sampford Arundel:** the sandy ford; held by Roger Arundel in 1086. *[DB]*

W   **Savernake:** from British river-name, Severn.

W   **Seagry:** brook with sedge growing by it.

A   **Sea Mills:** mills near to the sea.

S   **Sedgemoor:** moor where the sedge grows.

W   **Seend:** from British river-name, Semnet.

S   **Selworthy:** the enclosed farmland by the copse of sallow. *[DB]*

S   **Shallowford:** the shallow ford.

S   **Shepton Beauchamp:** the sheep-farm; held by Robert de Bello Campo, 1212. *[DB]*

S   **Shepton Mallet:** the sheep-farm; held by Robert Mallett in the reign of Henry I. *[DB]*

S   **Shepton Montague:** the sheep-farm; held by Drogo de Montacute, 1086. *[DB]*

W   **Sherston:** farm on the steep ridge. *[DB]*

A   **Shirehampton:** possibly the sheriff's village.

W   **Shrewton:** the sheriff's manor.

W   **Silbury:** the hill where the sallows grew.

S

s   **Simonsbath:** Sigmund's pool.

A   **Siston:** Sige's farm. *[DB]*

s   **Skilgate:** the opening on the boundary. *[DB]*

W   **Slaughterford:** the ford by the blackthorn trees.

A   **Sodbury:** where Soppa lived, by the hill, perhaps with a British camp. *[DB]*

s   **Somerton:** the farm to which people and livestock were taken in summer. *[DB]*

A   **Stanton Drew:** the farm with stoney ground; held by Drogo, 1225. *[DB]*

A   **Stanton Prior:** as above; held by the prior of Bath. *[DB]*

W   **Stanton Fitzwarren:** as above; held by Fulco, son of Warini, 1196. *[DB]*

W   **Stanton St Bernard:** as above; the name is of a local family settled from France.

W   **Stanton St Quintin:** as above. *[DB]*

A   **Staple Hill:** hill where a post stood.

A   **Stapleton:** farm by the post.

W   **Steeple Fitzpayne:** from the church with a steeple and the name of the Norman overlords. *[DB]*

s   **Sticklecombe:** steep valley.

s   **Sticklepath:** the steep path.

s   **Stidham:** where a stud of horses was kept.

W   **Stitchcombe:** valley infested by gnats or midges. *[DB]*

   Stock/Stoke: The element *stoc* is found in a number of place-names. It originally meant a monastery or a hermit's cell; then, more generally, a holy place or a place with holy associations; finally, it became a general word for a meeting-place. In some of the names that follow it may well have had Christian associations in the past.

s   **Stocklinch Ottersay:** the once-holy place by the hill; held by John le Ostricer, the goshawk keeper in 1243. *[DB]*

s   **Stocklinch Magdalen:** as above; with the church dedication. *[DB]*

A   **Stockwood:** the dairy-farm by the wood.

S   **Stogumber:** the stock (see above) where Gumner lived. *[DB]*

S   **Stogursey:** the stock (see above) held by William de Cursy in the reign of Henry I. *[DB]*

S   **Stoke Pero:** as stock above; held by William de Pyrhou in 1243. *[DB]*

S   **Stoke Pewsey:** as stock above, with the name of the Norman family living there.

S   **Stoke-sub-Hamdon:** the stock under the hills with many villages.

W   **Stratford Toney:** the ford where the Roman road crosses the river; held by Ralph de Touney in 1242. *[DB]*

S   **Stratton:** the farm on the Roman road.

S   **Stratton-on-Fosse:** the farm on the Roman road; the Fosse Way was added later for clarity. *[DB]*

S   **Stratton over Fosse:** as above – the farm above the Fosse Way. *[DB]*

W   **Stratton St Margaret:** as above, with the church dedication. *[DB]*

S   **Street:** the town on the Roman road. *[DB]*

W   **Studley:** pasture for horses.

S   **Sutton Montis:** the southern part of the village; held by Drogo de Montacutis, 1086. *[DB]*

S   **Sutton Mallet:** as above; held by Robert Mallett meaning evil, in 1200. *[DB]*

W   **Swallowcliffe:** the slopes where the swallows were found. *[DB]*

A   **Swainswick:** Svein's dairy-farm.

W   **Swindon:** the hill with the pigs. *[DB]*

S   **Taunton:** farm on the river Tone.

W   **Teffont Evias:** the boundary spring; held by the Norman, Ewyas Barony. *[DB]*

W   **Teffont Magna:** the larger village by the boundary spring. *[DB]*

T - W

A **Temple Cloud:** cloud from an old British word meaning hill. Owned by the Knights Templar.

S **Templecombe:** the valley where the Knights Templar owned property.

A **Thornbury:** the hill where the hawthorne trees grew.

S **Thurloxton:** Thurlak's farm.

S **Thurloxhill:** Thurlak's hill.

A **Tickenham:** the farm of Tica's family. *[DB]*

W **Tidcombe:** the valley where blue or other tits were found. *[DB]*

W **Tidpit:** the hollow where tits were found.

S **Timberscombe:** the valley where timber was allowed to be cut. *[DB]*

A **Timsbury:** the timber grove. *[DB]*

W **Tisbury:** Tissa's place by the hill.

A **Tockington:** the farm belonging to Toca's family. *[DB]*

S **Tolland:** land on the river Tone. *[DB]*

W **Tollard Royal:** the hill, intersected by valleys, which belonged to the king (King John). *[DB]*

W **Trowbridge:** the wooden bridge.

W **Tytherington Kelways:** the farm of Tidhere's family; held by Elway de Cailleway in 1227. *[DB]*

W **Tytherington Lucas:** as above, held by Richard Lucas, 1202. *[DB]*

A **Ubley:** the glade in the forest where Ubba lived. *[DB]*

W **Uffcott:** Uffa's cottage.

W **Urchfont:** Eorhic's ford, or possibly spring. *[DB]*

S **Vellow:** apparently from an old English word for the rim of a wheel, possibly related to the lie of the land hereabouts.

S **Vexford:** the ford with fresh, drinkable water. *[DB]*

A **Vobster:** Fobba's hill.

S **Wadeford:** the ford that had to be waded.

34

w   **Walcot:** the cottage of the serfs. *[DB]*

s   **Wambrook:** the crooked brook.

w   **Wanborough:** the hill where apparently, though not certainly, there was a wagon. *[DB]*

s   **Wanstrow:** where Wrendel lived, by a tree. *[DB]*

w   **Warminster:** the church or monastery by the river Were. *[DB]*

A   **Warmley:** the forest glade infested with reptiles.

s   **Watchet:** the lower wood. *[DB]*

s   **Weare:** the place where there was a weir on the river. *[DB]*

s   **Wedmore:** the hunting-moor. *[DB]*

s   **Wellington:** the farm on the meadow where there was once a heathen temple. *[DB]*

A   **Wellow:** British river-name, Welwe.

s   **Wells:** the springs, now found in the Abbey grounds. *[DB]*

s   **Wembdon:** the stream for fishing. *[DB]*

s   **Wescombe:** valley by the western village or houses. *[DB]*

w   **Westbury:** the western hill-fort. *[DB]*

A   **Weston-super-Mare:** the western village above the sea.

s   **Weston Zoyland:** the western village on land by the river Zoy. *[DB]*

s   **Wheddon:** the wheat-valley.

s   **Wheddon Cross:** as above; where there was a village cross.

A   **Whitchurch:** the place with a church built of white stone.

w   **Whiteparish:** the parish with a white church.

w   **Whittonditch:** the white farmhouse on the Fosse Way.

A   **Wick:** dairy farm.

s   **Widcombe:** willow valley.

s   **Williton:** farm on the river Willett. *[DB]*

s   **Wilton:** farm with springs or wells. *[DB]*

w   **Wilton:** the farm, or village on the river Wilye.

s   **Wincanton:** farm on river Cale. *[DB]*

A   **Winscombe:** Wine's valley. *[DB]*

s   **Winsford:** Wine's place with a ford. *[DB]*

s   **Winsham:** Wine's village. *[DB]*

W - Z

A   **Winterbourne:** the stream that runs dry except in winter.

W   **Winterbourne Bassett:** as above; held by Alain Bassett, 1220. *[DB]*

W   **Winterbourne Dauntsey:** as above; held by Roger Daunteseye, 1242. *[DB]*

W   **Winterbourne Earls:** as above; held by Earls of Salisbury, 1250. *[DB]*

W   **Winterbourne Gunner:** held by a woman, Gunnora de la Mare, 1275. *[DB]*

W   **Winterbourne Monkton:** as above; held by Bocheville, France, who passed it to the Abbey of Glastonbury. *[DB]*

W   **Winterslow:** the burial mound of someone called Winter. *[DB]*

S   **Withypool:** the willow pool. *[DB]*

A   **Withywood:** the wood with the willows.

S   **Wiviliscombe:** Wifel's valley.

S   **Woolavington:** the farm of Wulflaf's family.

A   **Worle:** the wood of the wood-grouse. *[DB]*

S   **Wookey:** trapping-place for animals.

S   **Wrantage:** the pasture for stallions.

ASW **Wraxall:** the place with buzzards or other birds of prey.

W   **Wroughton:** the farm on the twisting stream. *[DB]*

A   **Yate:** the gap or pass. *[DB]*

A   **Yatton:** the farm in the gap (also suggested that it might be the farm where the cuckoo was regularly heard). *[DB]*

S   **Yeovil:** a doubled river name. The original name of the river was the British Gifle, written as Givele in the Domesday Book. The 'G' seems to have been sounded as 'Y', and after the *DB* period began to be written as Yeo. *[DB]*

S   **Yeovilton:** the farm on the river Yeo or Gifle. *[DB]*

W   **Zeals:** where the sallow grows. *[DB]*

S   **Zoy:** British river-name.

ABSON BOOKS

THE DAY OUT Series 1, 2, 3 and 4 – all £1.50 with Derek Jones and Gwyn Richards by arrangement with the B.B.C.

First Series: Clearwell, Clevedon, Devizes, Frome, Langport, Malmesbury, River Frome, Shaftesbury, Stroud, Sherborne, Watchet, Wotton-under-Edge.

Second Series: Swindon, Porlock, Mells, Bradford-on-Avon, The Avon Gorge, Ilfracombe and Lundy, Sharpness Canal.

Third Series: Axbridge, Bridgwater, Chepstow, Bristol's Old City, Cirencester, Dorchester.

Fourth Series: Gloucester, Minehead and Dunster, Painswick, Taunton, Wells, Weston-super-Mare.

All with photographs and maps.

GARDENING MY WAY – £1.35 by John Abrams the gardening expert on HTV and the *Bristol Evening Post.*

ENGLISH COUNTRY SERVICE CRAFTS – £1.50. The crafts covered include hedging, dry stone walling, hurdle-making, thatching, scything, water-divining, wheel-wrighting and rural engineering.

KREK WAITER'S PEAK BRISTLE – 90p by Dirk Robson (Derek Robinson). The first guide to what the natives say and mean in the heart of the West of England.

SON OF BRISTLE – 90p by Dirk Robson. The second guide, with a special section on the famous BRISTLE 'L'.

BRISTLE RIDES AGAIN – 90p by Dirk Robson. The third hilarious guide to what the natives say and mean in the West of England with photographs of Bristol's statues passing contemporary comment in Bristolese.

 All available from booksellers or by adding 15p for the first copy and 8p per copy thereafter for packing and postage from the publishers, Abson Books, Abson, Wick, Bristol BS15 5TT.